The Wind Unwinds

poems by

Barbara Arzt

Finishing Line Press
Georgetown, Kentucky

The Wind Unwinds

ACKNOWLEDGMENTS

My appreciation to these editors for accepting my work:

VoiceCatcher ~ My Mother Who Danced for Nine Decades and Wheeling
Clementine Press ~ Alteration
Multnomah Art Center Catalogue ~ Affirmation

Publisher: Leah Maines
Editor: Christen Kincaid
Cover Art: Lorraine Sheahan, the author's mother. Photo by Maurice Seymour.
Author Photo: Paul Arzt
Cover Design: Leah Huete

Printed in the USA on acid-free paper.
Order online: www.finishinglinepress.com
also available on amazon.com

Author inquiries and mail orders:
Finishing Line Press
P. O. Box 1626
Georgetown, Kentucky 40324
U. S. A.

Table of Contents

To my grandma Anne Geiser Sheahan
poet and painter

Searching Dusty Leaves

I'm a bit unglued from sifting through
my mother's jam-packed house
where everything I touch is a decision.
Empty cardboard boxes
surround a crowd of books
stacked inside these mantel shelves
half their lives and all of mine.

From the wall they pester me,
dignified and decorated,
ragged and inviting.
Their flowery spines scan my eyes:
Browning, Byron, Keats,
Shelley, Wordsworth, Yeats.

Should I pack them out with haste
and no communication? Or waste some time
languishing inside their brooding covers?
One by one I peel them from the painted shelves,
pan the yellowed fly-leaves for lineage
alive in signature:
Albert, Anne, Louise, Edward, Frank, Bernice.

I fan the pages, breaking free mementos left—for me?
Anne's poems on torn-paper-scraps,
pressed violets and aster,
flourished bookmarks,
pastel paintings,
a Copperplate love letter fading. A shock!
of golden locks tied with yellow ribbon.

For a moment I lose pace and wonder if my pining
is childish or misplaced. Is there something more
without roots or shoots or ribbons,
something I can't gather into a folio?

Most likely I've been tossed by wafts
of old leaves and dried leather toward
a craving to remain inside familiar chapters.

I run my fingers down a page
of great grandpa's crumbling bible
and feel the words he read
pressed into the paper.
Then choose another handsome cover,
moss green, debossed with gilded leaves
open it to anywhere, and there:

A poem and a drawing, a figure seated near a fire,
half-hidden by a wall of books and more around the mantle.
Below, the poem, "Confessio Amantis":
When do I love you most sweet books of mine?....
I slide into Le Gallienne's honeyed affirmation,
wipe my crowded tears and mark the boxes:
Old Books <u>SAVE</u> .

My Mother Who Danced for Nine Decades

The flowering plum
that was so optimistic
has fallen in pink rusty piles.
Everything is falling,
my hips, my tits, my mother,
her ragged smile
like the crack in her pelvis
they said had been there for a while
from when she shouldn't have lived alone
and I was ignoring the rotten food
and her talk of moonlight walks,
that stash of Hershey's next to the corn chips
next to the jug of vodka—
I only pour two drinks no more—

At 92 she was still performing,
and brought down the house
at the village Arts Center
with a crisp tap dance and a smile
that made you believe. At 94 I found her
unable to get off the bathroom floor.
But she'd fallen for years
got up and kept on fighting
like Punchy, her father, did in the ring,
and that's where she got her strong bones
that gave me this heart of calcified pity.
Will tears ever find their way through,
or did her ambition crowd the soft spaces
so that I cry poems instead?

Alteration

The deaf trees roar and strain
against their shallow roots.
Wind, delirious, wraps the house
and turns it upside down.
Day is night and
night is day
and my mother sees devils
dance on the ceiling.
She's been hearing a symphony
way too long and
doesn't like the music.
Sitting in bed she reaches out
to gather the floating dollars.
I'm unsure who is more undone
me or this woman I don't recognize
who swears she's at the theatre
but I'm almost certain
we're somewhere near Christmas
in my own living room, though
the tree looks very different this year
and a constant fire blazes.
So I make believe summer
in shorts and no sleeves.
I'm good at pretending
all sorts of things
like the measure of time
on my own drifting skin but
I can't deny the glassy gaze
that slides across my mother's face.
Between the storms the wind unwinds
and rights the twisted trees.
Into the silence my idle talk,
a lyrical mist,
seeps below her wrinkled skin
to where our blood runs as one.

Part of Me

When somebody asks what you want for your birthday
and the first thing you think is, *for mother to die*
you probably shouldn't say that out loud
(or write it in a poem) even if she never
got up to make you breakfast
showed you how to bake a cookie
or fix your too curly hair.
(She cut it tight to your head
and sent you off to school because
To hell with what those people think!).

Mom's been in our living room
for 10 months and 12 days.
So instead of flying off to Thailand
driving up the Alcan Highway
or over to the Steens
we take trips (in shifts) to Safeway.

I can't stop grinding my teeth,
and my flexing jaw reminds me of James Dean
or Elvis Presley (no, not Elvis, he had no muscle)
I remember the first time I saw him
on the Ed Sullivan show.
I loved it, how angry Ed was,
arms crossed tight against his chest
as if he could hold back the revolution.
No matter how he yelled into the mic,
the audience wouldn't behave.
Is that why he was angry? Or was it because
the lid blew off the kettle and
he wasn't part of the steam?

Mom doesn't know what day it is
or to take the pills that keep her alive
but she remembers Elvis,

that night in black and white. These nights
I look over the landing at her in the living room
sitting on the edge of the bed
staring into the fire
telling stories to the flames
that never grow tired .

I joined the Marine Corps in World War II to get out of Whiting Indiana

How the doors of the train closed
on the tanks and distillation towers
and opened two thousand miles later
to the smell of Gardenia and lemon.

Dad and I met at Toni's restaurant in Santa Barbara during the war.

How gentle he was the first time we made love
at the Fairmont hotel in San Francisco.

But last night when I peeked over the railing
she was standing under a lighted lamp
examining a picture of my father
seated at a holiday table holding a cigarette,
his dark eyes sparkling at so much time,
and I watched her kiss his face,
then wipe the picture with a pajama cuff,
but it wasn't enough and she kissed it again,
and I broke at the waist as she whispered
I miss you so much.

Forgiving Fate

My smile
fell off
in December
and ran away
with the rain
probably
clear to
the ocean
by now
carelessly
bobbing free
or hooked
and flipped
upside down
to a frown
too small and
ugly to keep
cast back
to the chuckling deep
having learned
its salty lesson
will crawl to this
solemn place
if it takes its time
and the stars align
there's a chance
it will fit
my face.

Respite in Red

My mother likes the same thing for breakfast
in the same chair every day so I march
from the kitchen with coffee and toast
V8 and two poached eggs.
She never has much to say
so I sit and watch the skin cells
floating through a sunbeam.
Even the dust is no longer my own
and I'm working again full time
a nurse, a cook, an accountant,
a cleaner, a hostess, a maid,
as if my home were a *bed and breakfast*
I tend with a pasted smile not like
that airy sparkle-toothed beam on the
face of a stranger I passed in the park
who wore a green buttoned coat
hair shaved high above the ears
long strands of red from the top
of her head shot up like a silken flame
catching the sun and my fancy.
I managed to look in her eye with a grin
that grew as she flitted by and
wanted to shout out a *thank you!*
But she wouldn't have understood why.

Good Friday

It does seem rather still today
maybe because the stock market's closed?

At least quiet trickles down.
On Sunday I'll see a one man show

and I like the guy already
cause he goes to work on Easter.

I don't believe that Jesus rose
only that he died.

Dad Died on a Flag Day
easy to remember.

We thought we'd all get over it
but mother never did.

Good Friday would be a good day
to die with two billion people mourning.

My sister thinks we should
save some cash to spend on

the poison pudding and drift away
as easily as dogs.

They'll sell it on the street by then
a *Boomer Bye Bye* medley

in five nostalgic flavors
for only an arm and a leg.

My Mother Too

My lazy heel scrapes the path
as I walk back to the house
where mom doesn't hear
her slippers shuffle
like snare drum brushes
across the hardwood floor.

The late Autumn breeze is cold
but not cruel like The Hawk
that cuts across Lake Michigan
and through the Windy City.

I don't recall how old I was,
maybe 14 or 15,
but I remember where I stood,
frozen by the fireplace,
when mom recalled that night
on the Navy Pier—
a date with a guy she knew.

Never let a boy touch you, she began.
We danced for a while. He held me close.
I was so innocent, so naive.
He said we needed to go outside
there was something he had to show me.

He had a knife
so I didn't fight
when he shoved me into the car.

At the trial I told the truth
but they twisted my words
until even my father
didn't believe me.

The guy went free.
Mom gained a memory
that sharpened her
vision and cut her loose
from kindred arms
and tightly held opinion.

It's something I try
not to think about.
But, you know,
if I hadn't up and left
for the west coast,
I would never have met
your father.

Shifting Current

Seasickness is the nausea you feel
when the motion seen conflicts
with the motion sensed by the inner ear
somewhere inside the tubular loops
alongside the sea shell- shaped Cochlea.

The first five days out I puked over the side
of dad's troller that summer of '74
when coho sold for 68 cents a pound
Chinook just over a dollar,
when beer was just beer and the number one song
was "The Loco-Motion".

I left the Chicago Ballet that year—
Adieu to all that miserable beauty and corps of sweaty swans—
to slip through the jaws of the Newport jetty,
me and dad and the Duna rolling
early morning over the bar
and into another magnificent terror.

When the fish finder's sound waves flashed back
blips and blops we'd lower the outriggers
and bait the main lines every two feet
with colorful, glow-in-the-dark, skirted hoochies,
then troll at nine knots to lure schools of salmon
as go-go dancers lured loose men
with a flip of fringe and a shimmy.
Really? How could they? The fish, I mean,
be tricked by those rubbery pretenders
of herring, minnow, pilchard and squid.
Then we'd wait for the bells on the poles
to break the conversation
we were having in our heads,
and when it did, dad would jump—
with more than useful enthusiastics—

spitting his boiled egg into the spume,
he'd set the gurdies squealing,
both our heads tipped over the side,
hoping for black lips as fins broke water.

Then I'd leap to the stern away from the gaff hook
swung into the pounds of each flopping fish
clubbed and tossed with a slimy slap
(and sometimes I wished it was him)
against the glittered bulwark.
My job was to slit them from anus to throat
and toss the guts to the screeching gulls
who followed the boat with the other groupies—
cormorants, sea lion, and shark.

Now, forty years later, he's dead, my dad,
but I googled the Duna and she's still fishing
out of Puget Sound. I've been to sea only once
since then, on a night snorkel off Hawaii,
but every summer I have this compulsion
to swim in cold green rivers, and I do.

In My Mother's Attic
(For Sarah)

a steamer trunk unlocks with a key
tied to a crumbling leather handle.
A musty smell wafts from the crack
I jostle to open like a tall thick book.
Hanging racks and cloth compartments—
a green and yellow floral pattern—
are faded from waiting
more than a hundred years.

In the top drawer, wrapped in a kerchief,
letters written by my grandma
aboard the steamship St Paul
on her way to Europe in 1921.
This trunk traveled with her.

In the middle drawer:
beaded bags and baby shoes,
a fine tulle wedding veil, silk stockings,
castanets, Paris opera glasses, and
great-great grandma, Eliza Geiser, in an oval frame.

Tiny pearl buttons that weight lacy sleeves
on great grandma's evening dress
reflect back to her in this black feathered hat
the heels of these high buttoned shoes
knocking the boardwalk in Baker City.

In the bottom drawer a black velvet cape
and a brocade smoking jacket with
great-granddad's initials, AG,
embroidered on the cuff.
I slip my hand into the pocket
to find grains of tobacco wedged in the seam,
nestled there since before the Great War,
before basketball or the automobile,
but not before the mixing of seeds
was sifting its way toward me
in this folded moment,
far from those I never thanked.

The House Is So Sad

Slumped in the passenger seat
of the van, I watch as my husband
lifts dad's gear out of the trunk.
Things I'd rather not see
glance off the side mirror glass
as they're passed
onto the loading dock
at the Salvation Army:
bags of duck decoys, fishing poles,
golf clubs, gold pans, that sou'wester ....

I can barely look at it now,
the house,
a sign stabbed into the lawn:
For Sale. Yesterday,
a photographer came
to take lifeless pictures
so strangers can gape
at the echoes.

I kept the ax, the wedge,
and the peavey
because too much of me
still sits on a stump
watching my dad
fall tall timber.

Open-House-Sunday
they'll come, the curious,
in their dirty sneakers
to march up the soft fir stairs
into the bedrooms, commenting
on the color of the walls,
not one of them seeing
two sisters race, squealing,
up that same staircase
to call dibs on the rooms
they'd grow up in.

Even the ghosts are glum.
Bloated with memory
they float to the rafters
pressing against the ridge-beam
like ragged breath held
too high in the chest.
This defense of the past
can't continue, they'll see.
Then, perhaps, they'll just
move in with me.

Sand Dabs

I've come to the Oregon coast
to fill up on poems
fished from the jaws of this jetty.

But they don't come around
when you need them
So far I've lured only a flounder.
These swooping gulls could tell a tale,
but lyrical seems so old school.

What made me think they'd come flying
over the Newport bridge
under this noonday sun
to shadow-paint my pages?

It isn't a lack of material
that's keeping them at bay:
driftwood, foghorn, lighthouse, dingy,
any object that avoids the subject will do.

I've tried casting between the lines
but just when I think I might have one
it slips off the hook and I'm left
with a creel of amnesia.

My groping sends them into hysterics.
There's one now paddling by
dressed up as a seal,
barking a laugh as it slaps the water
and disappears under the surface.

They've researched the art of camouflage
have doctorates in elusion,
assuming the changing shape of fog,
the moon's breath in a wave
or the language of this wind-bent reed
scribbling a script in the sand
translated by the imagination.

Wheeling

I've taken to talking to myself
especially here in the park:
What is it about this time of year
that makes the crows shit oysters?
It isn't that way in the summer
when they're slinging berry pies.

Where's the sun they promised?
I'm wet and my hands are freezing
trying to write in this tiny notebook
using my head as an umbrella,
as if I had something to say. Maybe
that inflated notion will get me
off the ground. It will take a lot of hot air
cause I'm weighted down by my mother.
Today we'll go for lab work
and she won't want to walk
so I'll wheel her down the clinic hall
and up to an IV station
where they'll check for
a poem in her blood.

Bliss

My song is
way too
blue.
I want to
swap notes
with that
sparrow who
doesn't
have a clue
his tune
is just
a peep.
Filling the air
like he
doesn't care
he's only
an accident—
the perfect
picture
he has
no need
to paint.

Sing, Sing, Sing

My sister came by to sit with mom so
I walk up the street with a notebook
to an un-named pie shop in the village
thinking I'll order lemon balm tea
and grab a piece of a poem.
But when I get there it's open mic song night.
A singer is making her way to the stage.
She looks fragile and timid and that
makes her thinness seem thinner.
I hold my breath and feel myself shrinking.
The guitar begins the intro to "Wave",
that slippery stoned bossa nova
that makes you yearn for key lime pie.
I see her lips moving. Is she singing?
Someone tells her to get close to the mic.
But that just magnifies what isn't there
like zooming in on a blurry picture.
Every hoped for wave
is a feeble pianissimo.
The consonants are absent
but I can swallow that.
It's the vowels that are the problem,
the way they trip
around the notes
like drunken dancers
never falling on the pitch.
How is that even possible?

I could run to the bathroom
or slip out the front door,
but it's right next to the stage.
Oh god, she's bending down
with the mic in her hand
to turn up the amplifier!

The screech stops but
my ears are ringing.
I think she's singing in Portugese,
but I guess I'll never know.
We applaud, she swells and beams.

A woman named Beverly takes her place
to sing "Blue Moon" and "I'll Get By".
Four measures in I develop a tick
that fiddles below my left eye.

At the end we all applaud loudly—
the performers seem bigger somehow—
not for the notes that fell short of music
but for dreams placed on the line
like a fragile poet reading out loud
every word on a scale.

All is as it should be,
quite the perfect evening,
completely unprofessional.
I think I'll come back next week
for this tender imperfection.
And maybe I'll work up a song.

Waiting for Lorraine

One last camellia bud, unopened,
hangs above a blanket
of fallen blossoms.
Imagine its surprise.

Will it be a surprise to wake
and find my mother still and pale
or will I be there waiting
for her last jagged breath?

Will she hover for a while like my father did,
raining roses and sweet peas down on me
before she moves away?

She'll barely have to turn
to find his kiss and, smiling,
she'll dance for him
as he sings *Sweet Lorraine.*

Thanks

I'd like to thank my first poetry instructor David Abel for giving me the courage to continue, to Judith Pulman for an energy that still spins, and to Donna Prinzmetal for showing me how to slim down. Thanks to poet and mentor John Brehm whose keen ear, humor, and loving heart made this chapbook possible. Thanks to my poetry group for their honest critique and unwavering support: Sue Einowski, Shelly Peters, Joe Thaler, with special thanks, to Shelley Reece. Thank you to Sarah, Louise, and Anna whose bright lights inspire, to my wonderful Joe and his piercing wit, with love to Chris who has shared the path, and to my ever generous Paul for being my bones for almost 40 years.

Barbara **Sheahan Arzt** grew up dancing in her mother's studio in Portland Oregon. She attended Indiana University School of Music on a ballet scholarship then went on to a 10 year performing career. She has lived in Chicago, Boston, New York, Los Angeles, and Mexico City. She returned to Oregon to teach dance, marry her husband Paul, and raise their son Joe in Carver Oregon on the banks of the Clackamas River. In 2012 she retired from dance. At the Multnomah Arts Center, she found Poetry and Calligraphy, and discovered that the pen could dance. Barbara is a member of the Portland Society for Calligraphy and her works have recently shown at exhibits in and around Portland. She continues poetry classes, workshops, readings, and meets monthly for critique with her poetry group. In 2018 she completed her first published collection, *The Wind Unwinds*, a chapbook inspired by the life changing experience of caring for her mother with dementia.

CPSIA information can be obtained
at www.ICGtesting.com
Printed in the USA
LVHW082214210419
614904LV00011BA/76/P

9 781635 348958